AF428942

VISIONS OF NATURE
EDITION II

Copyright © 2023 by Tyler M. King

All rights reserved. No part of this book may be reproduced or used in any manner without written permission of the copyright owner except for the use of quotations in a book review. For more information, address: tyler@tylerkingart.com

FIRST EDITION

www.tylerkingart.com

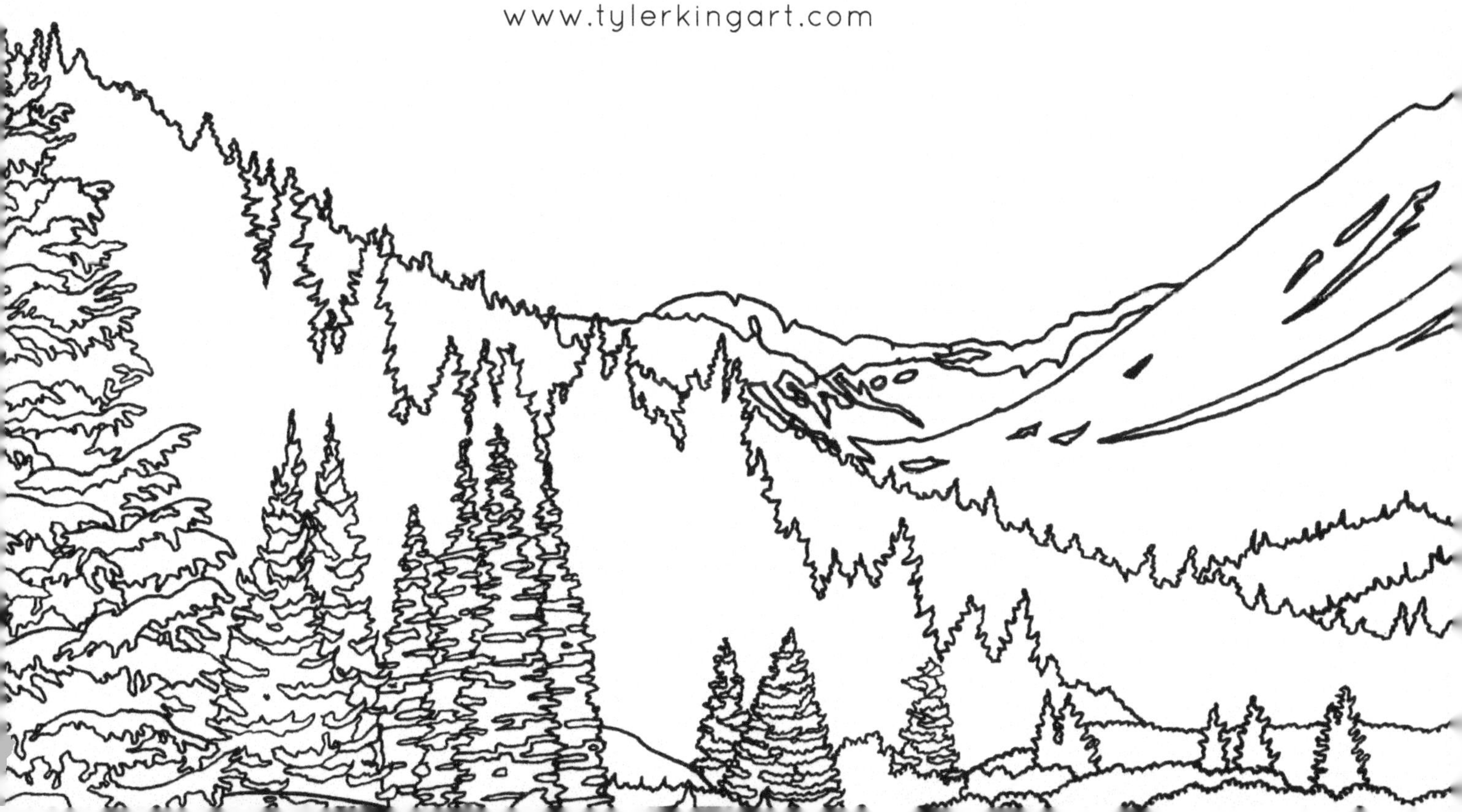

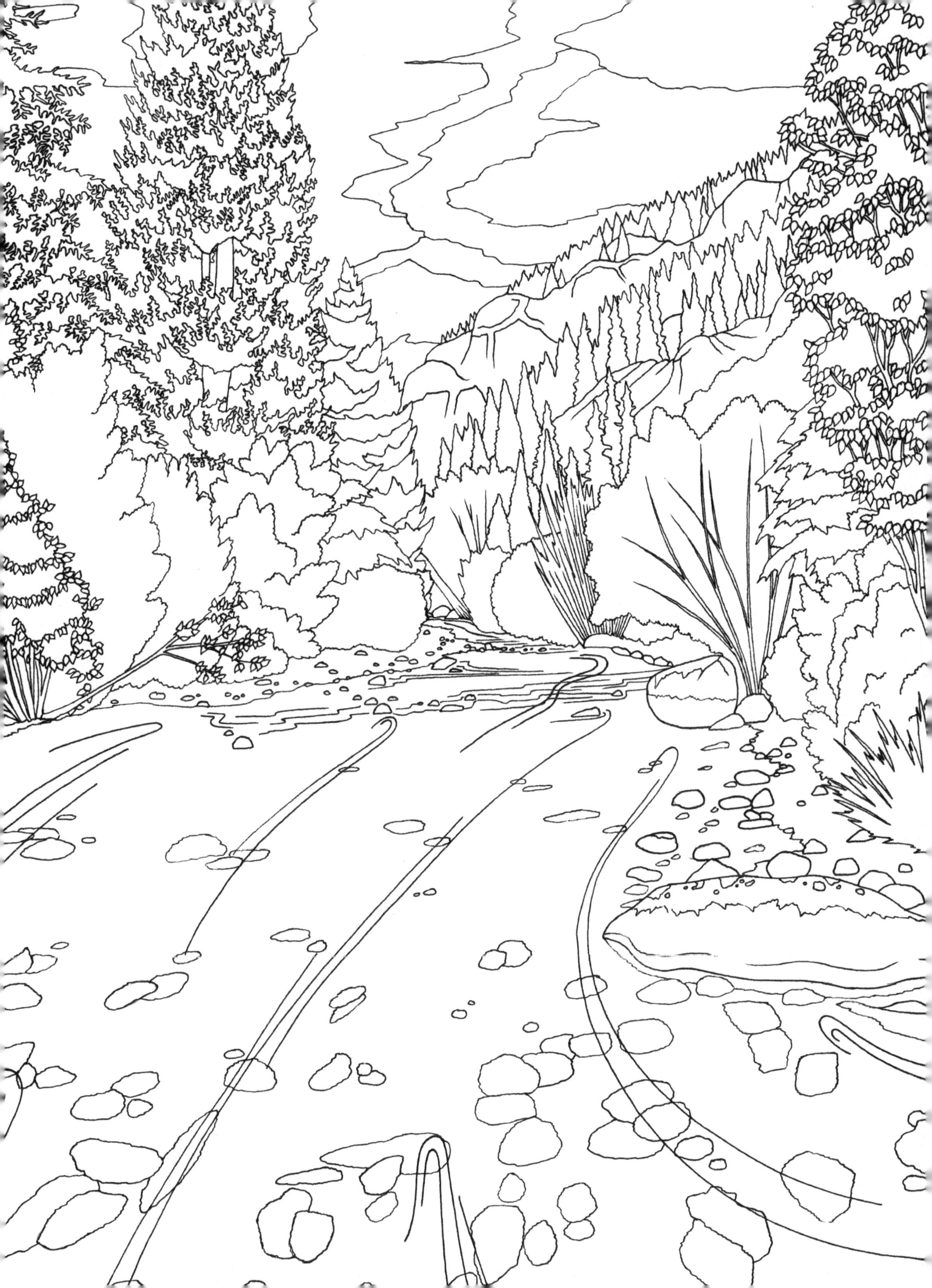

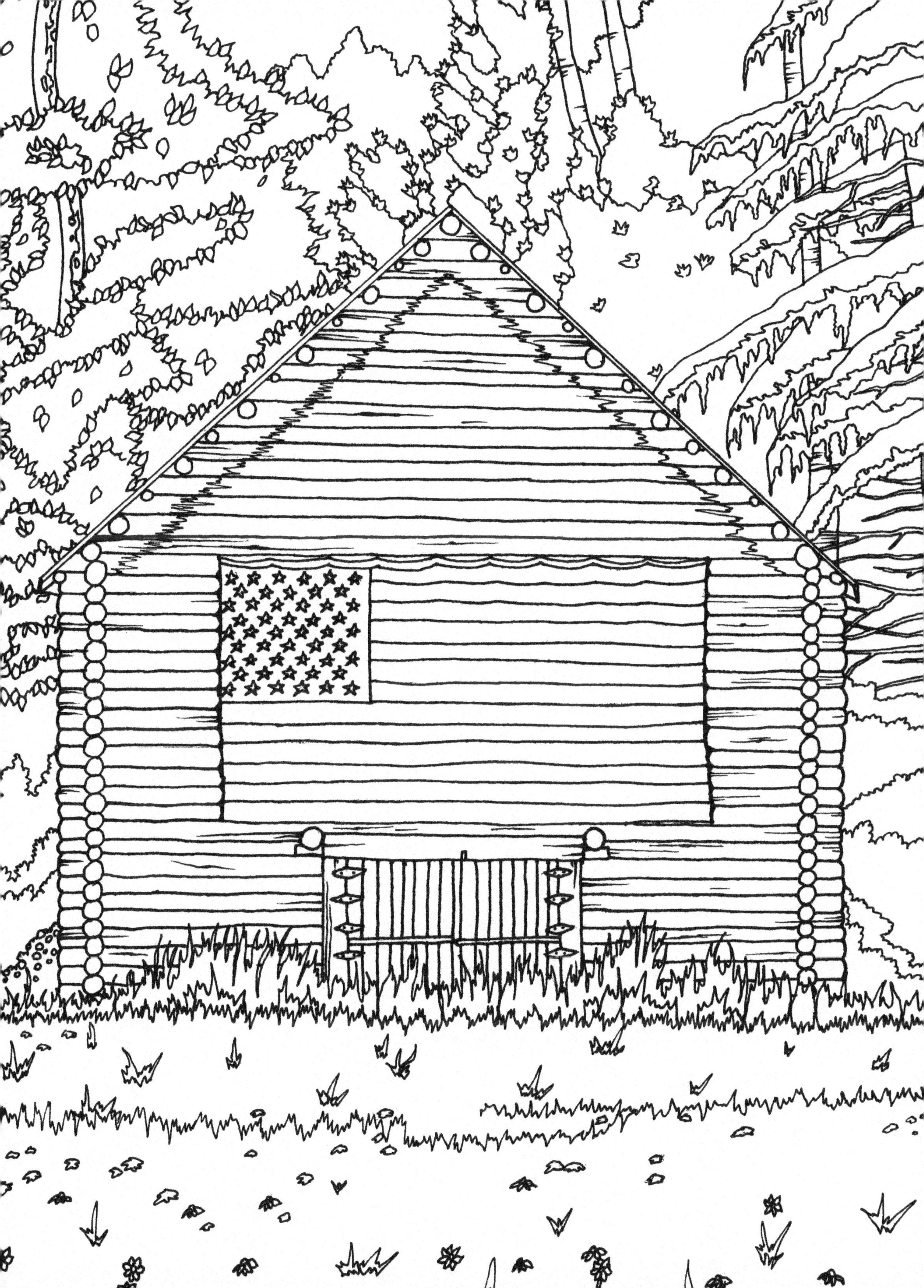

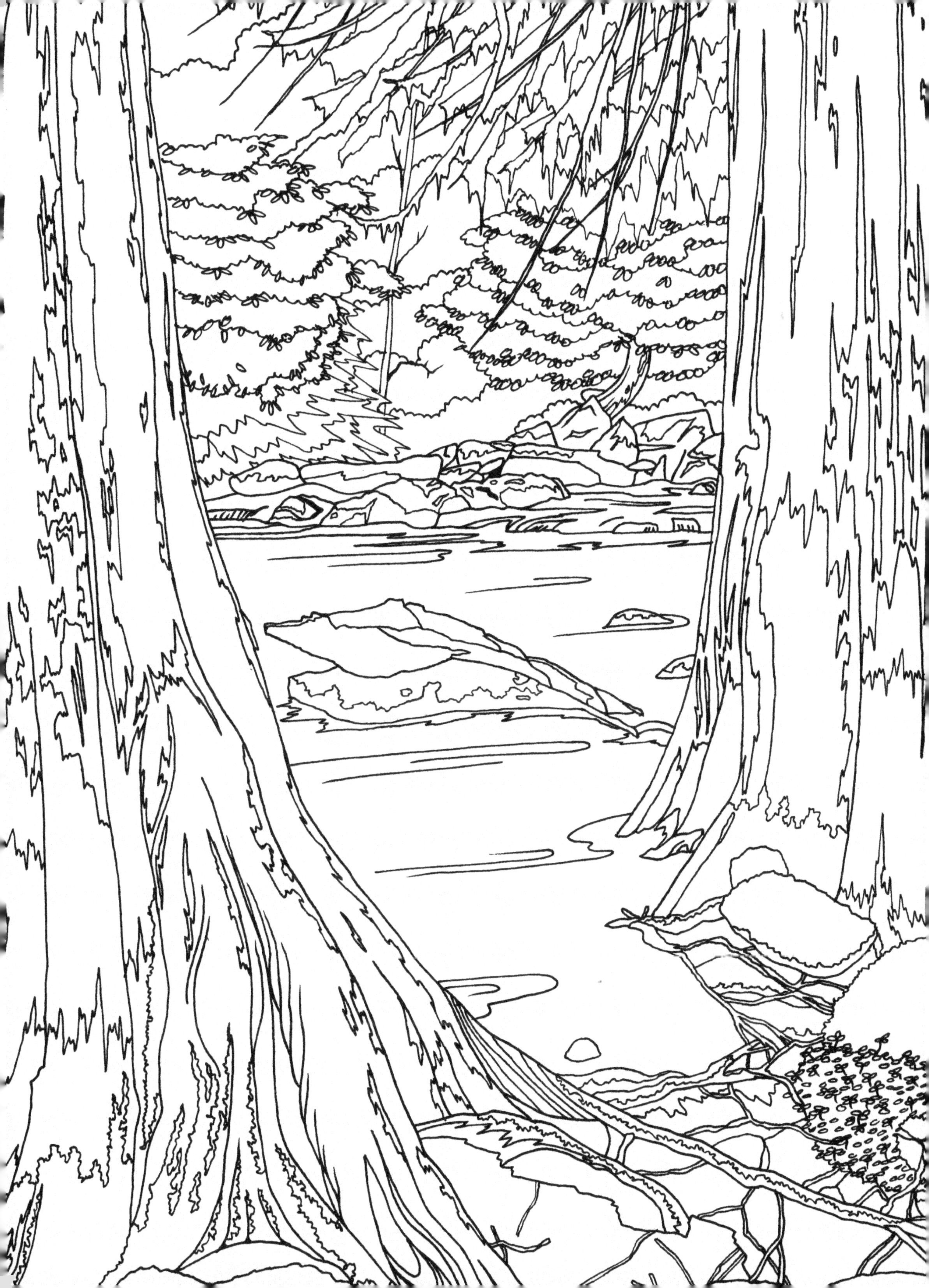

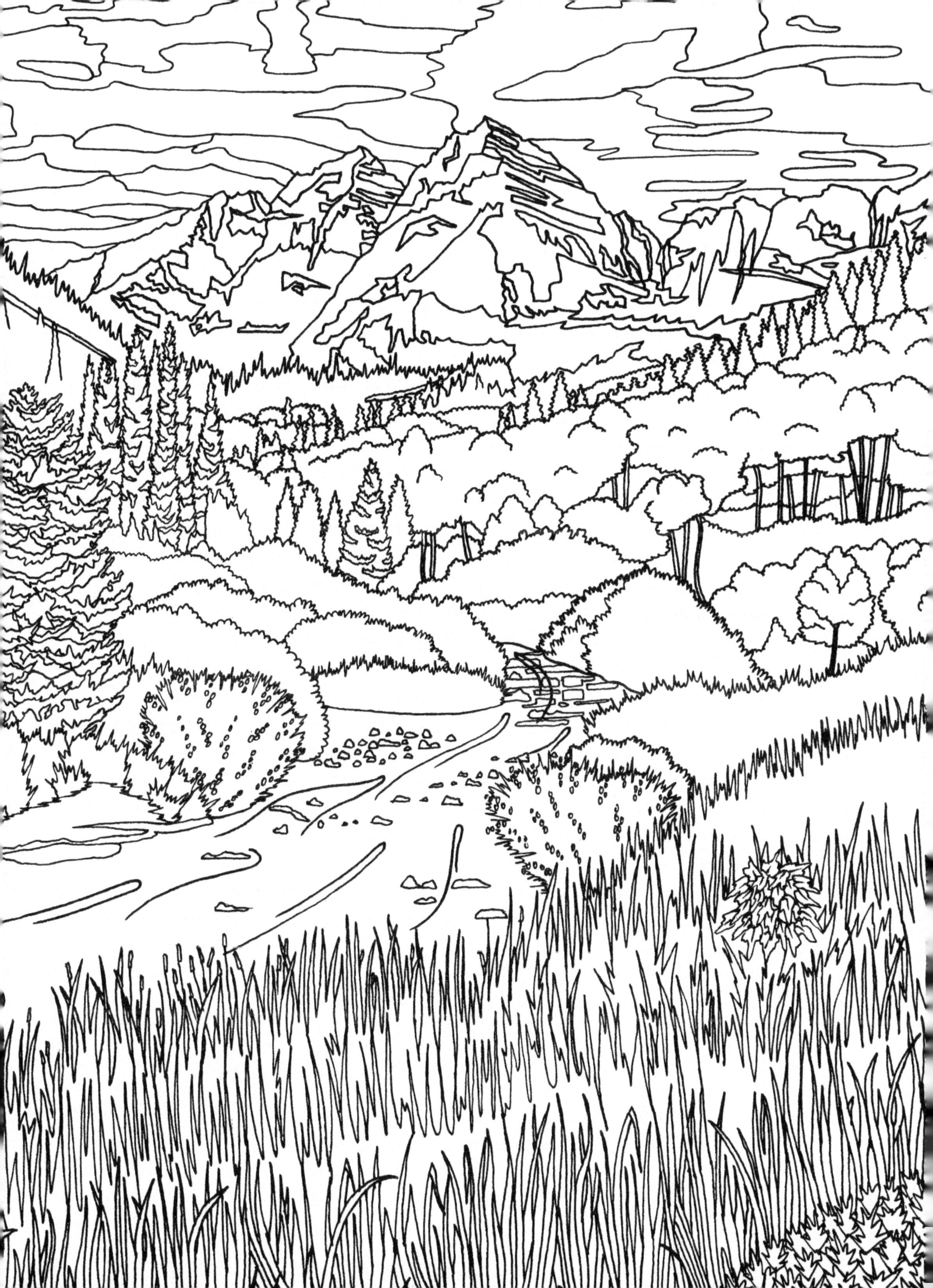

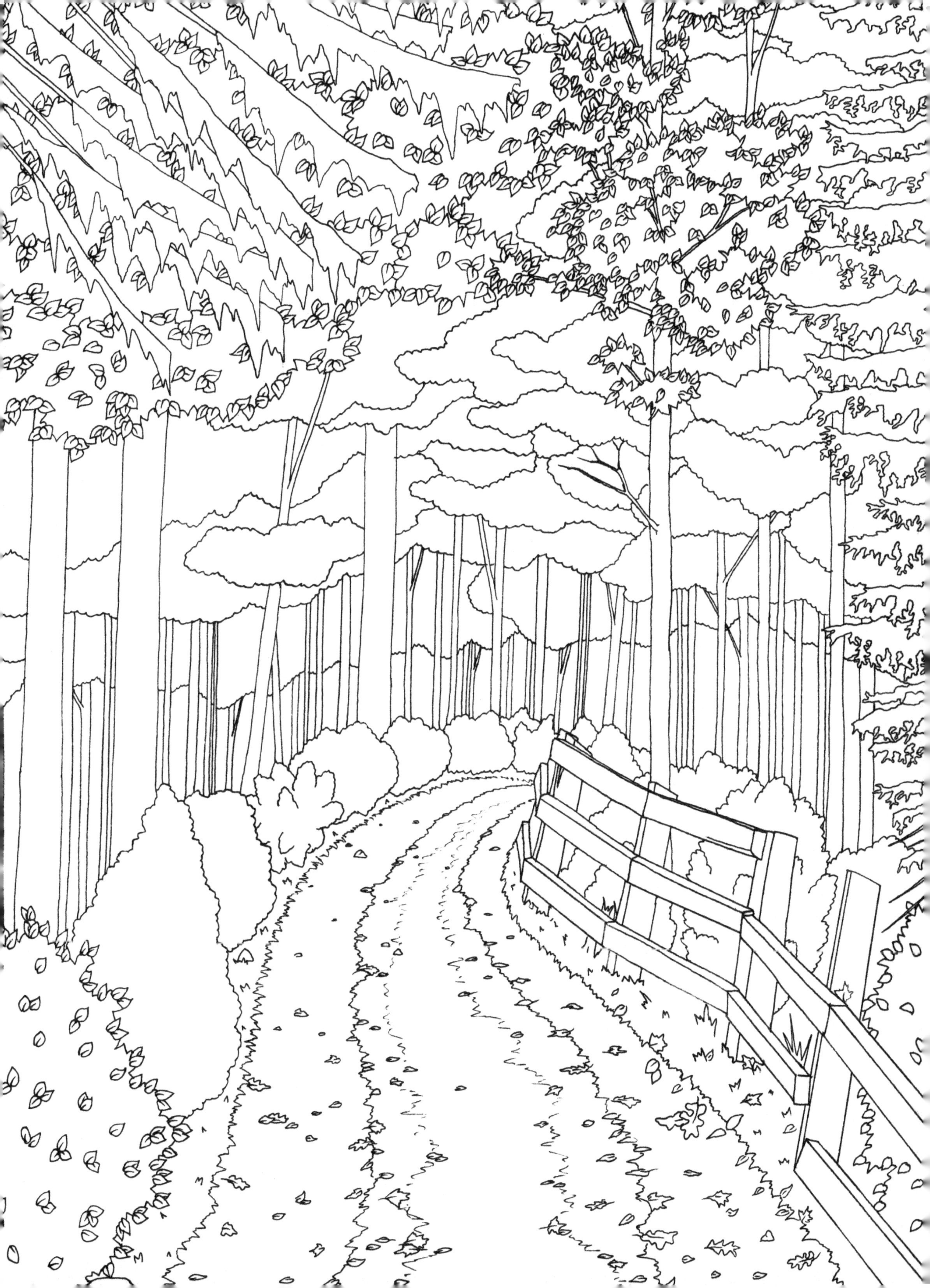

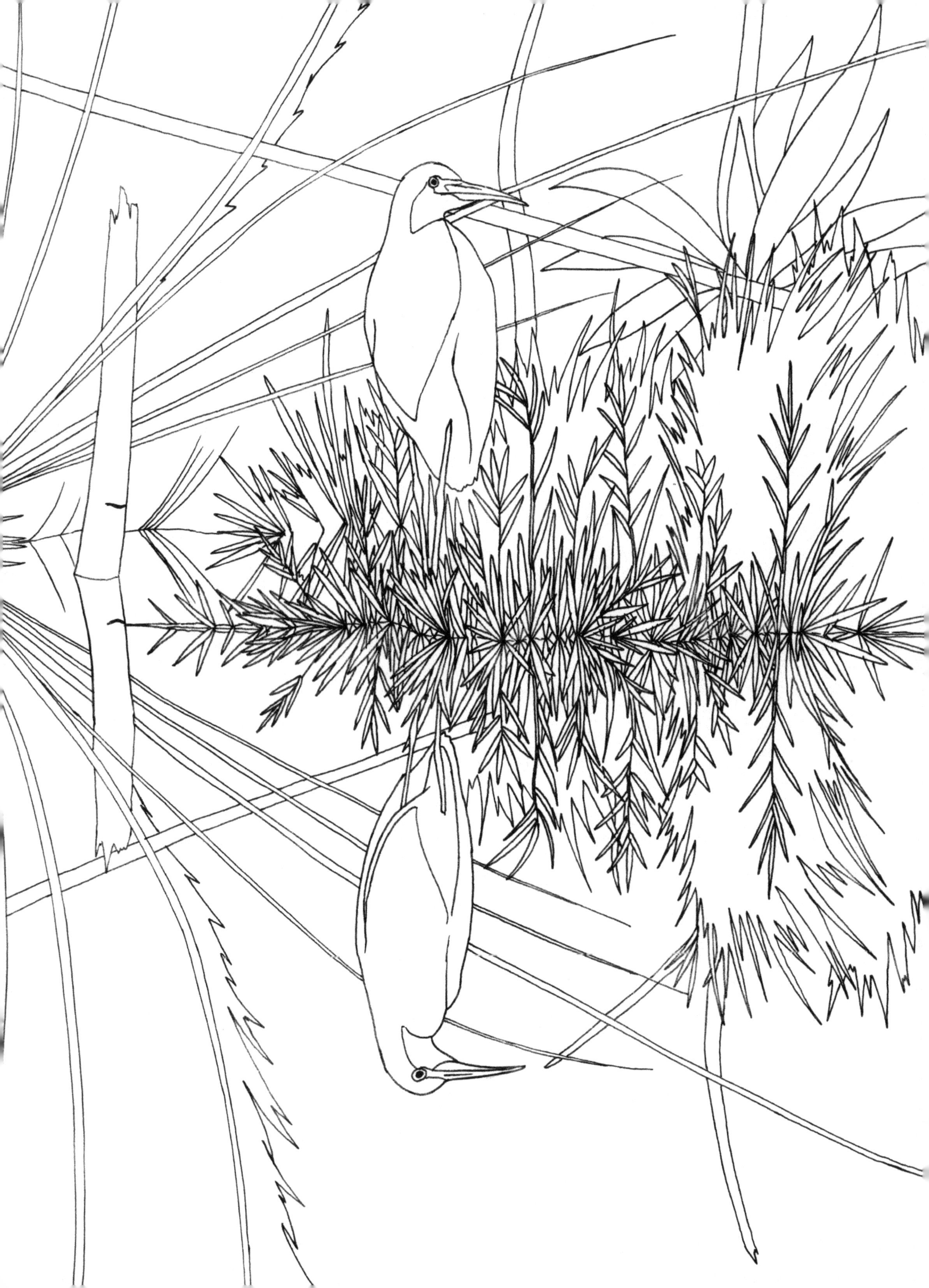

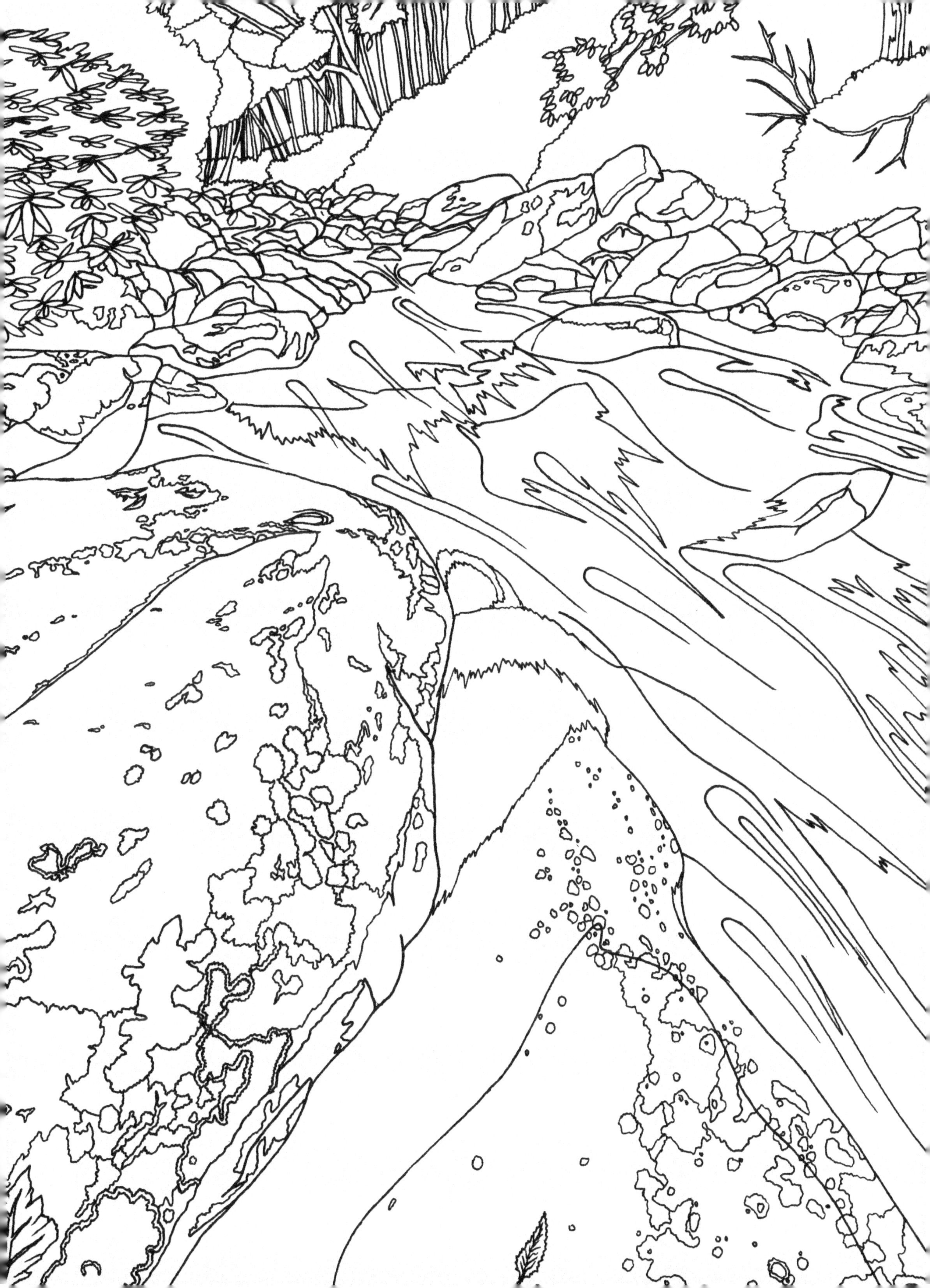

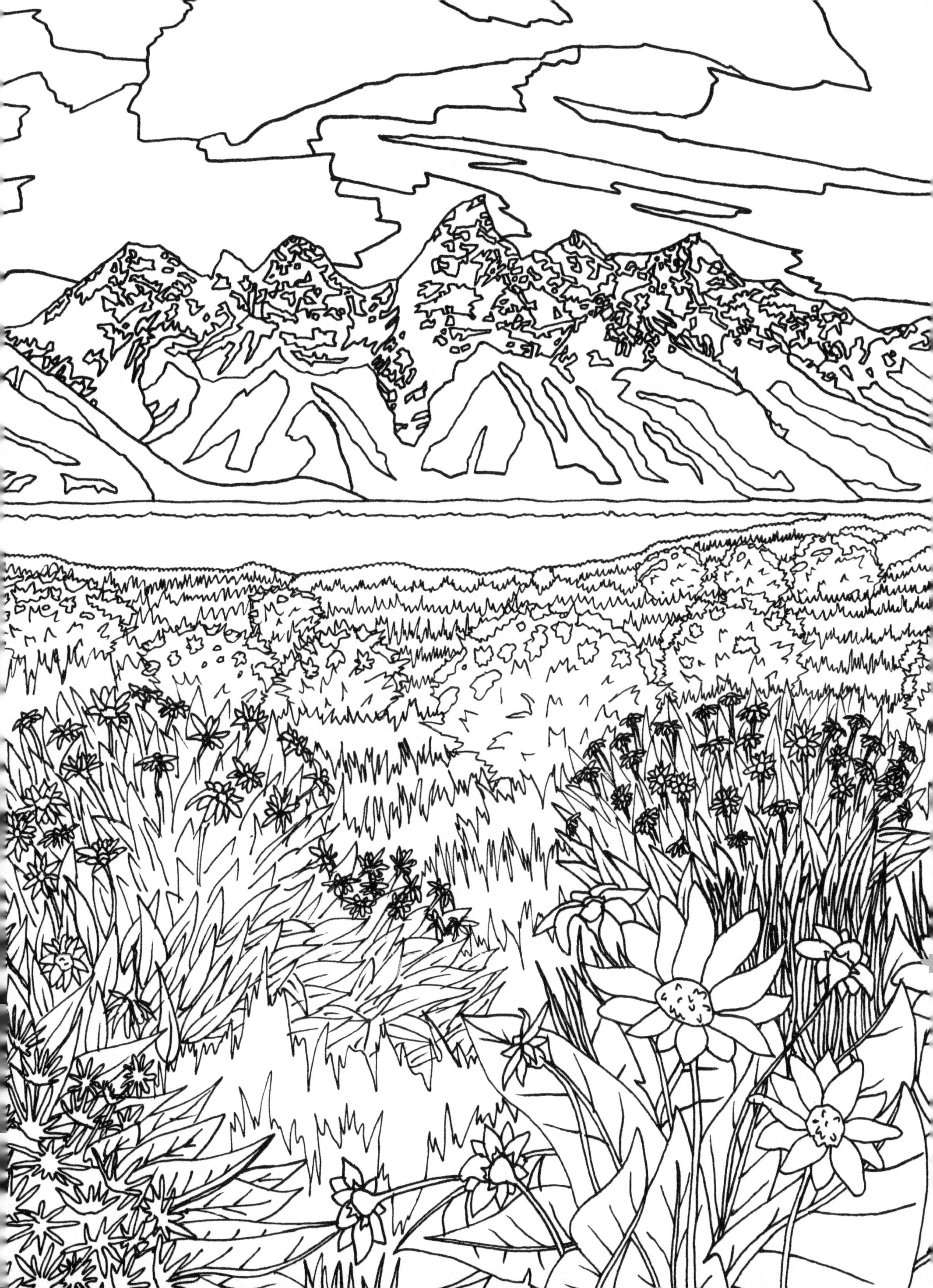

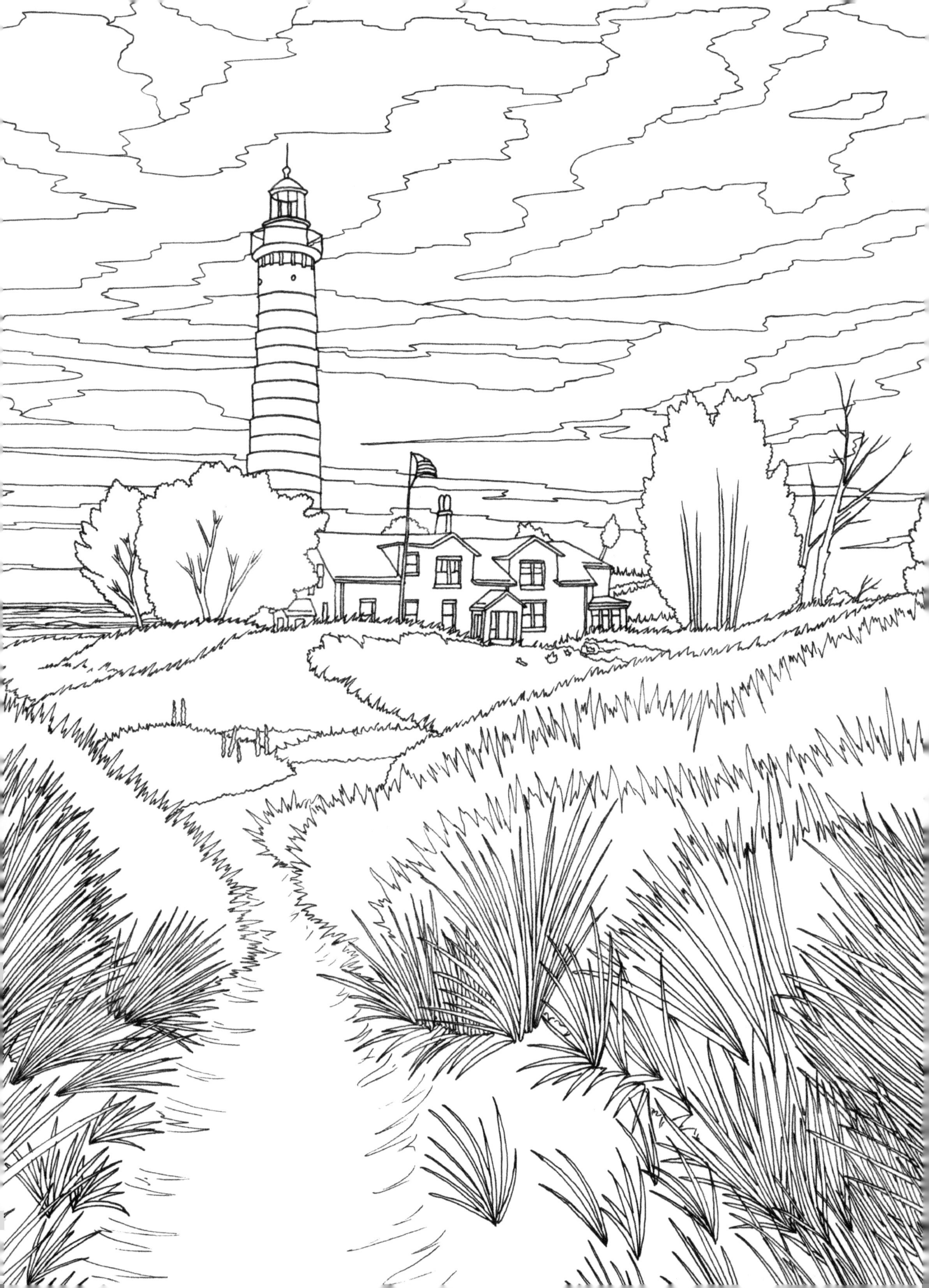

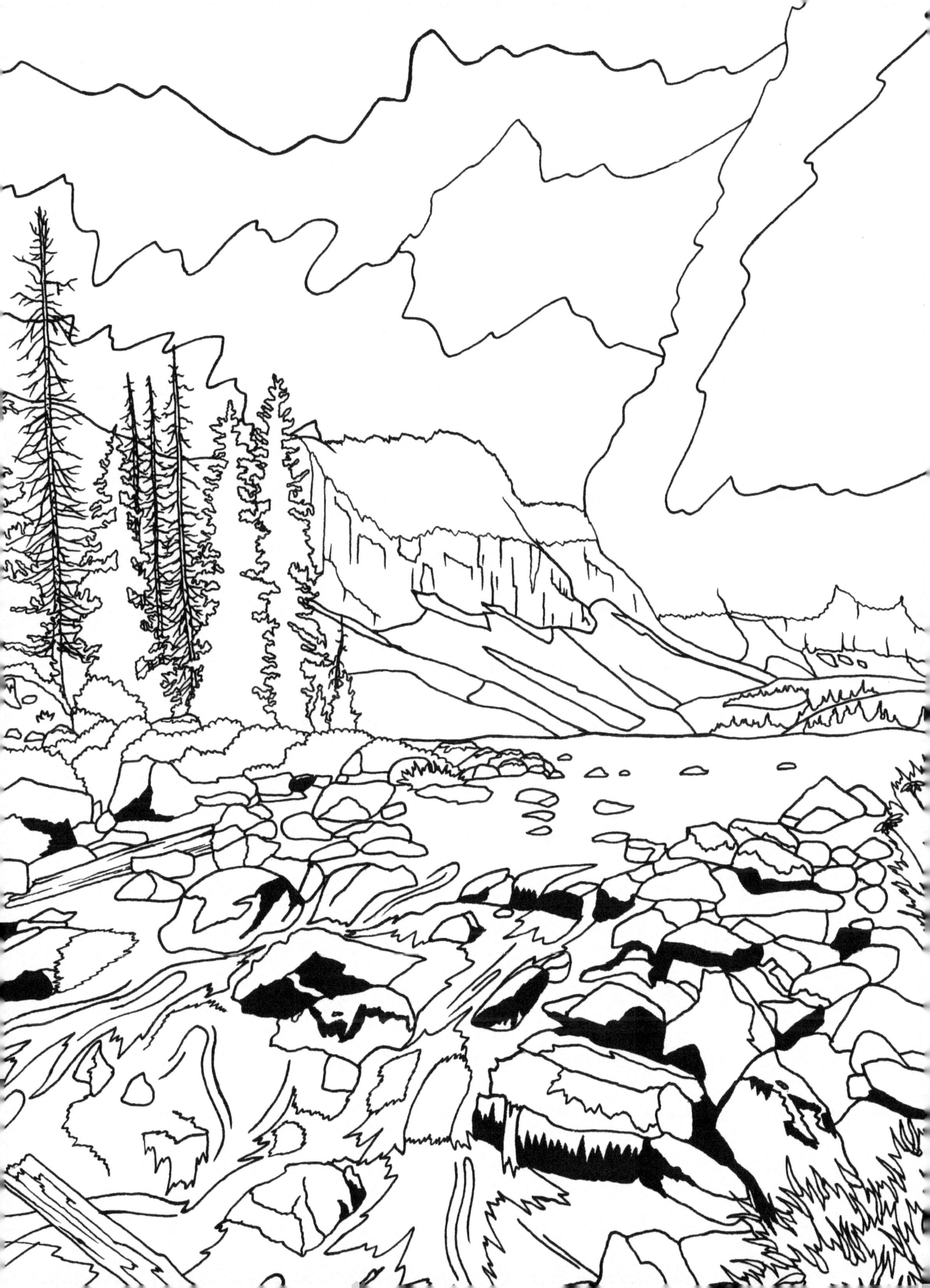

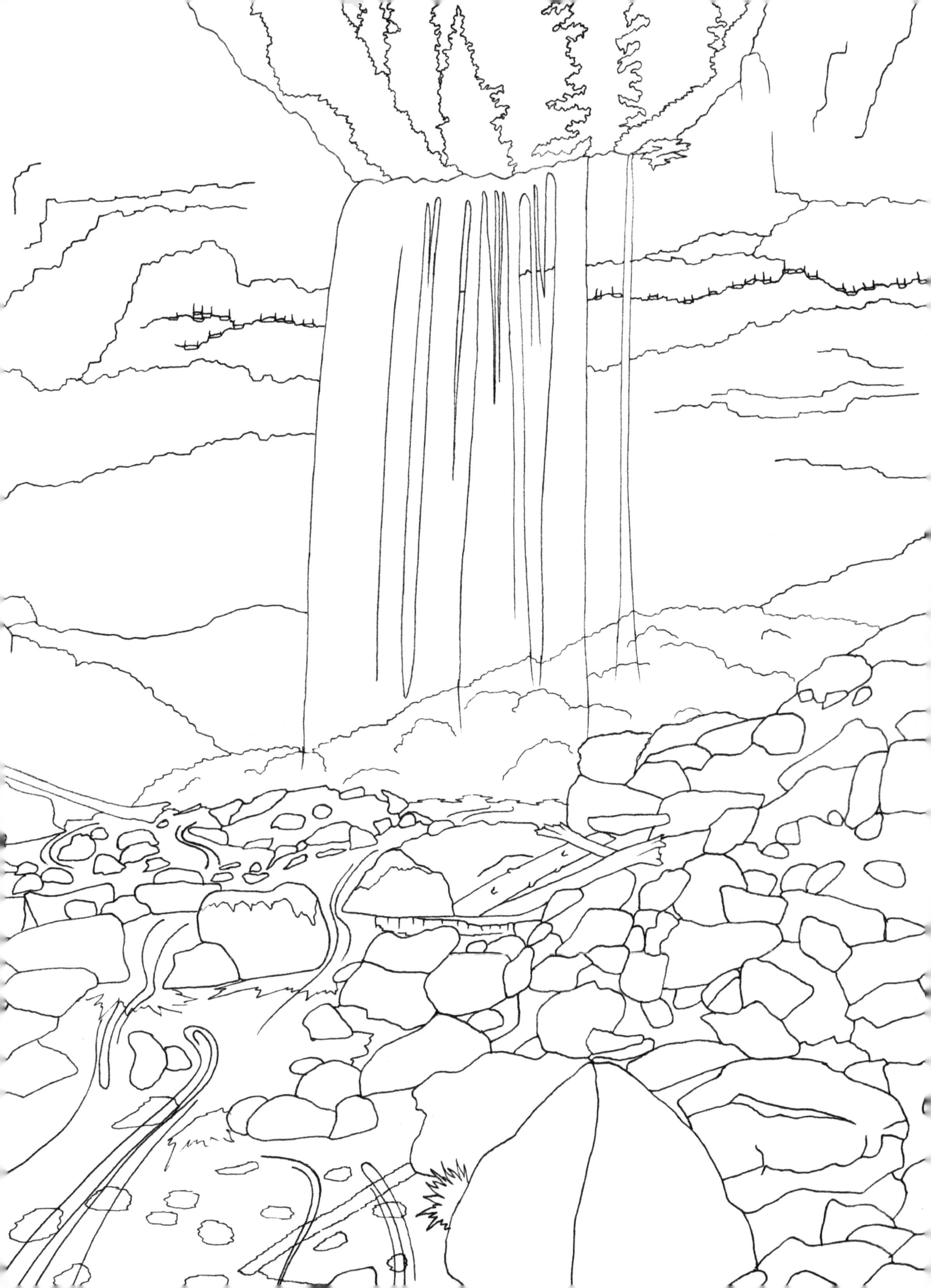

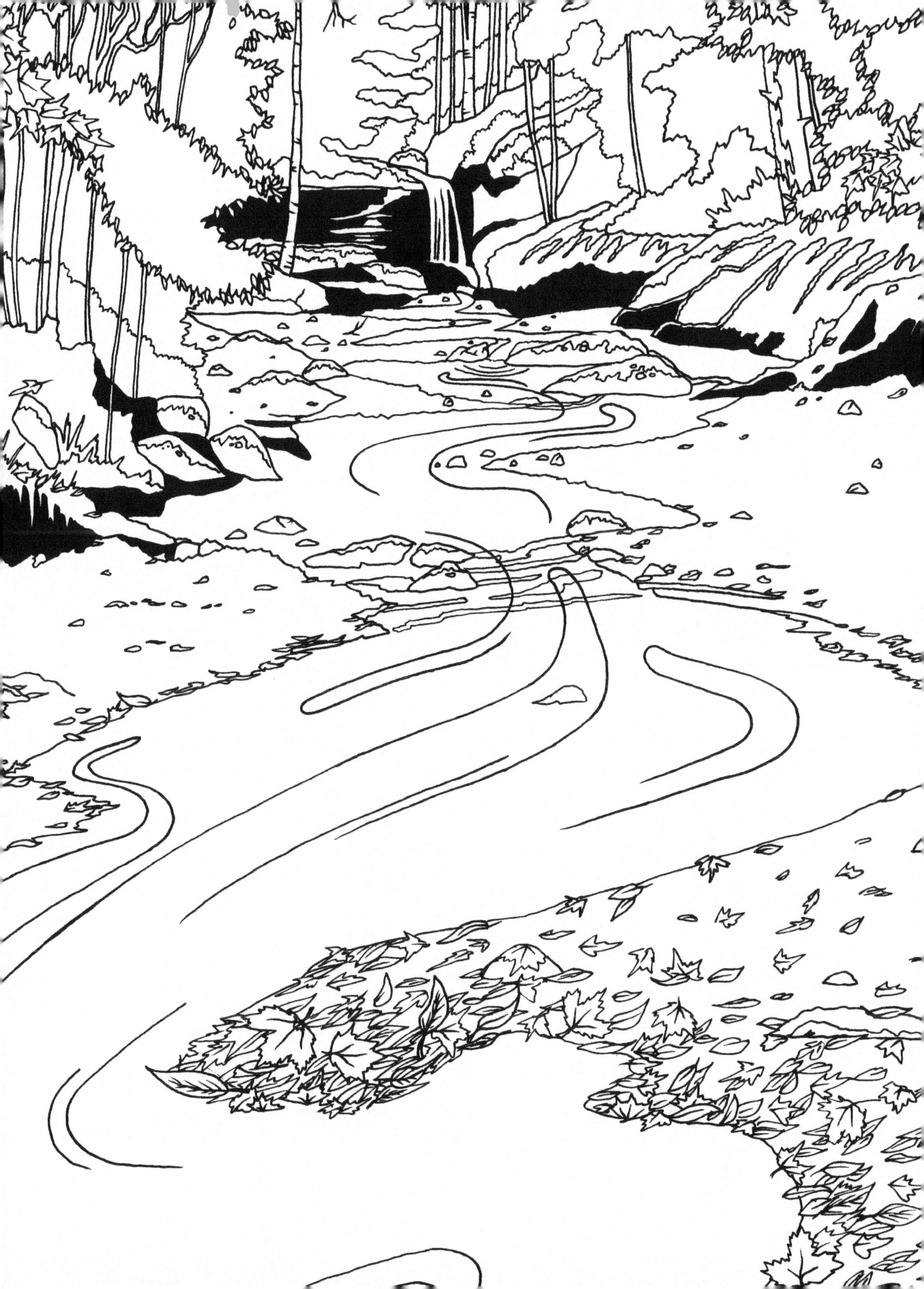

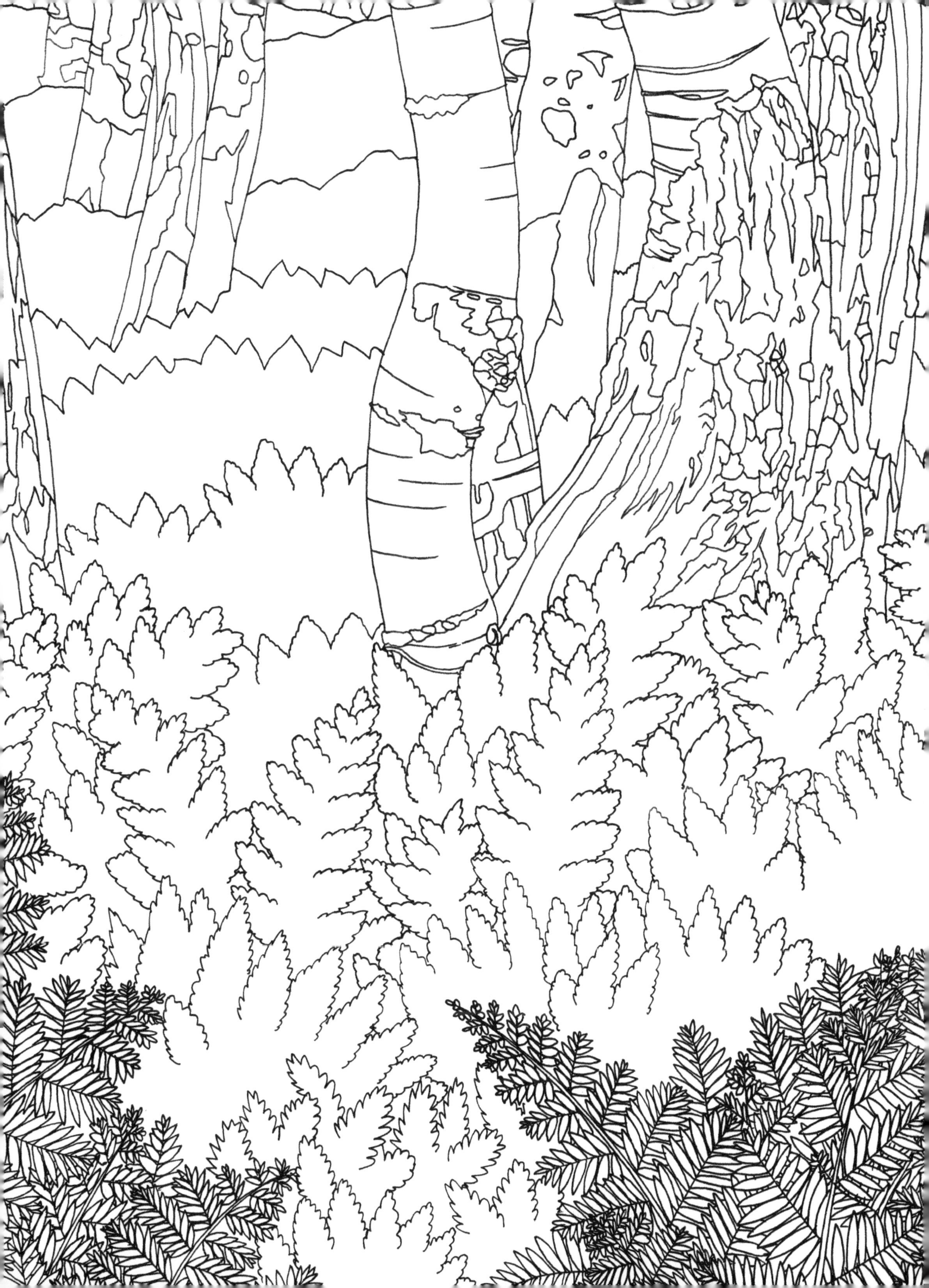

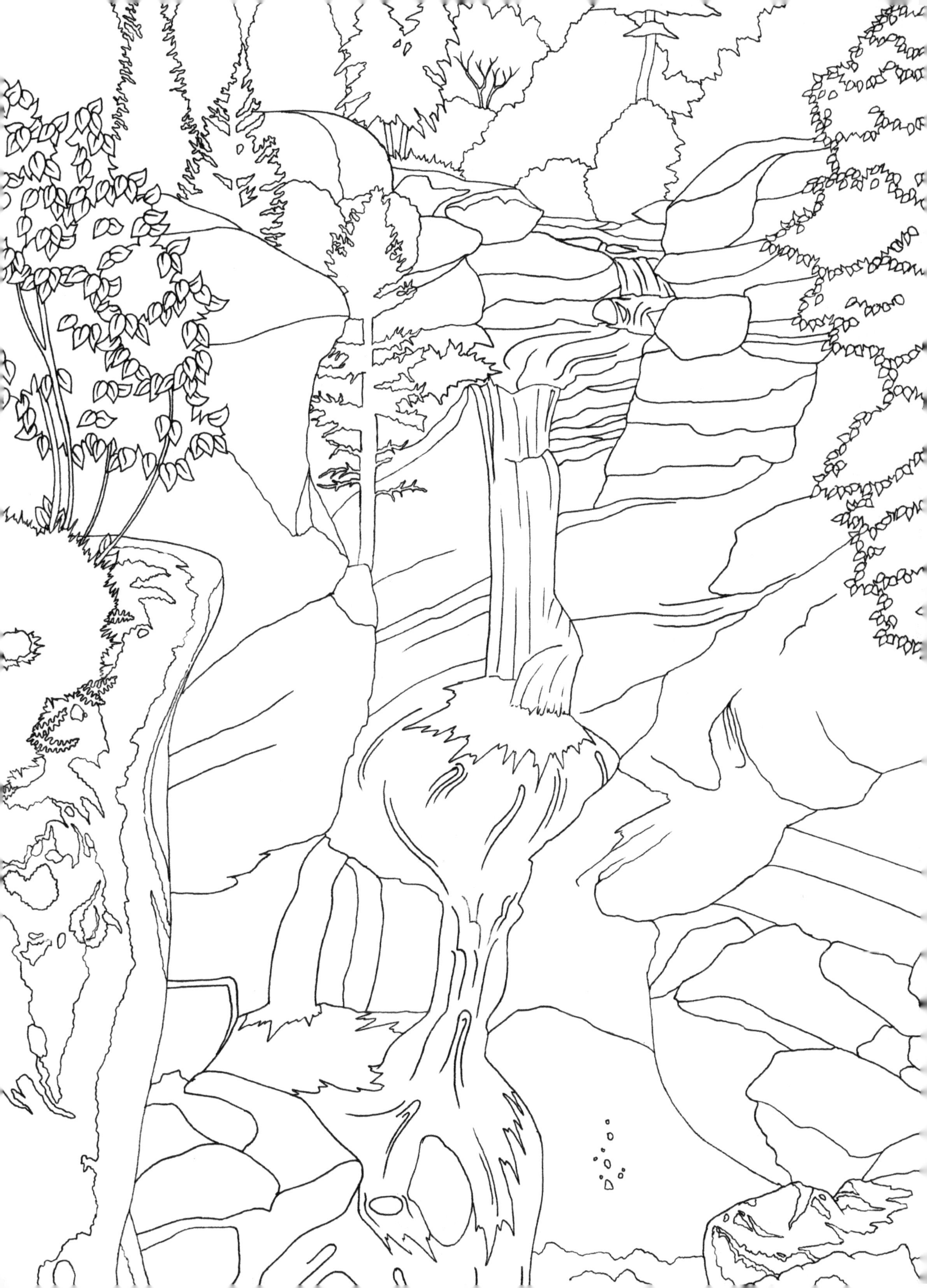

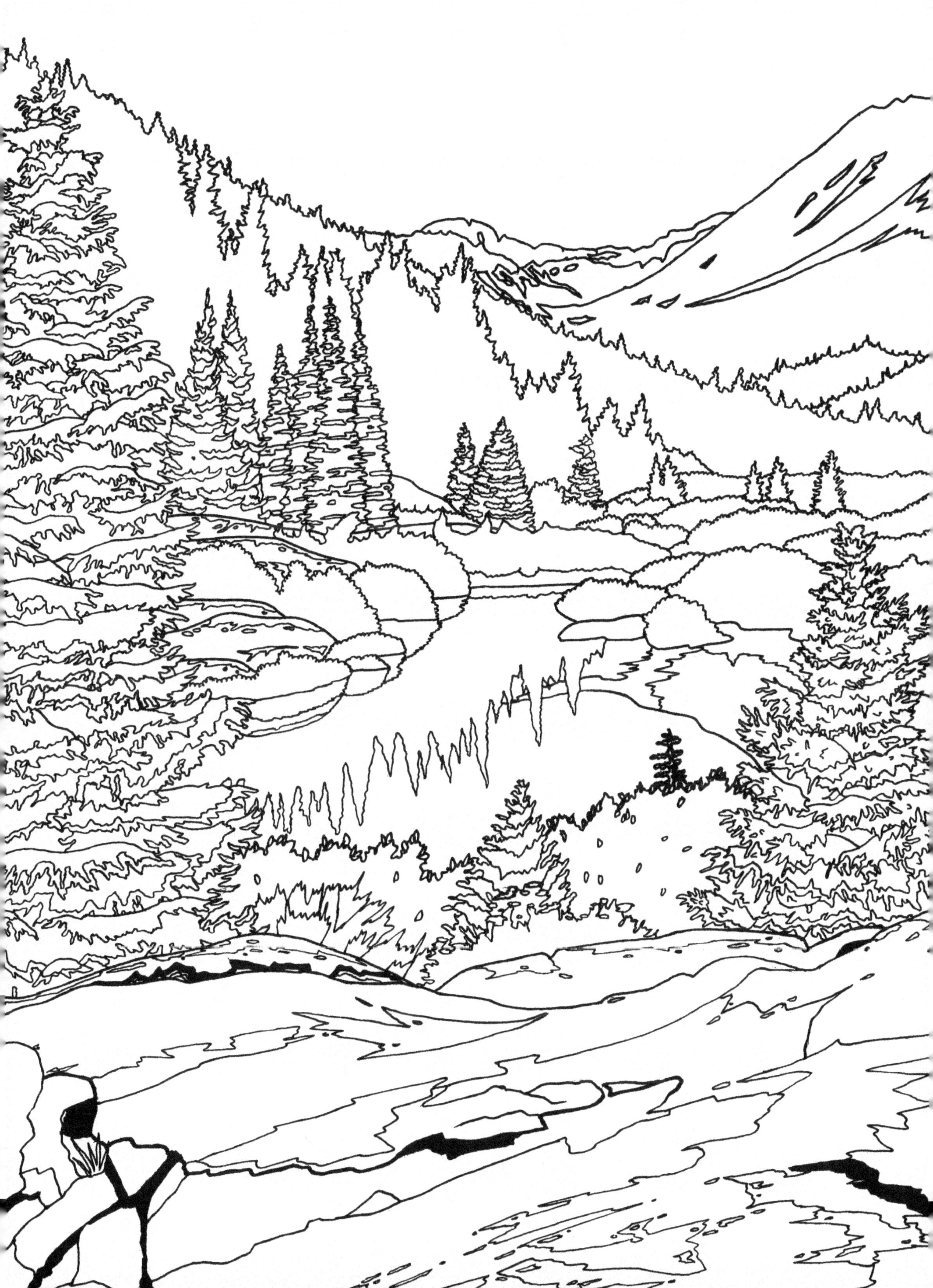

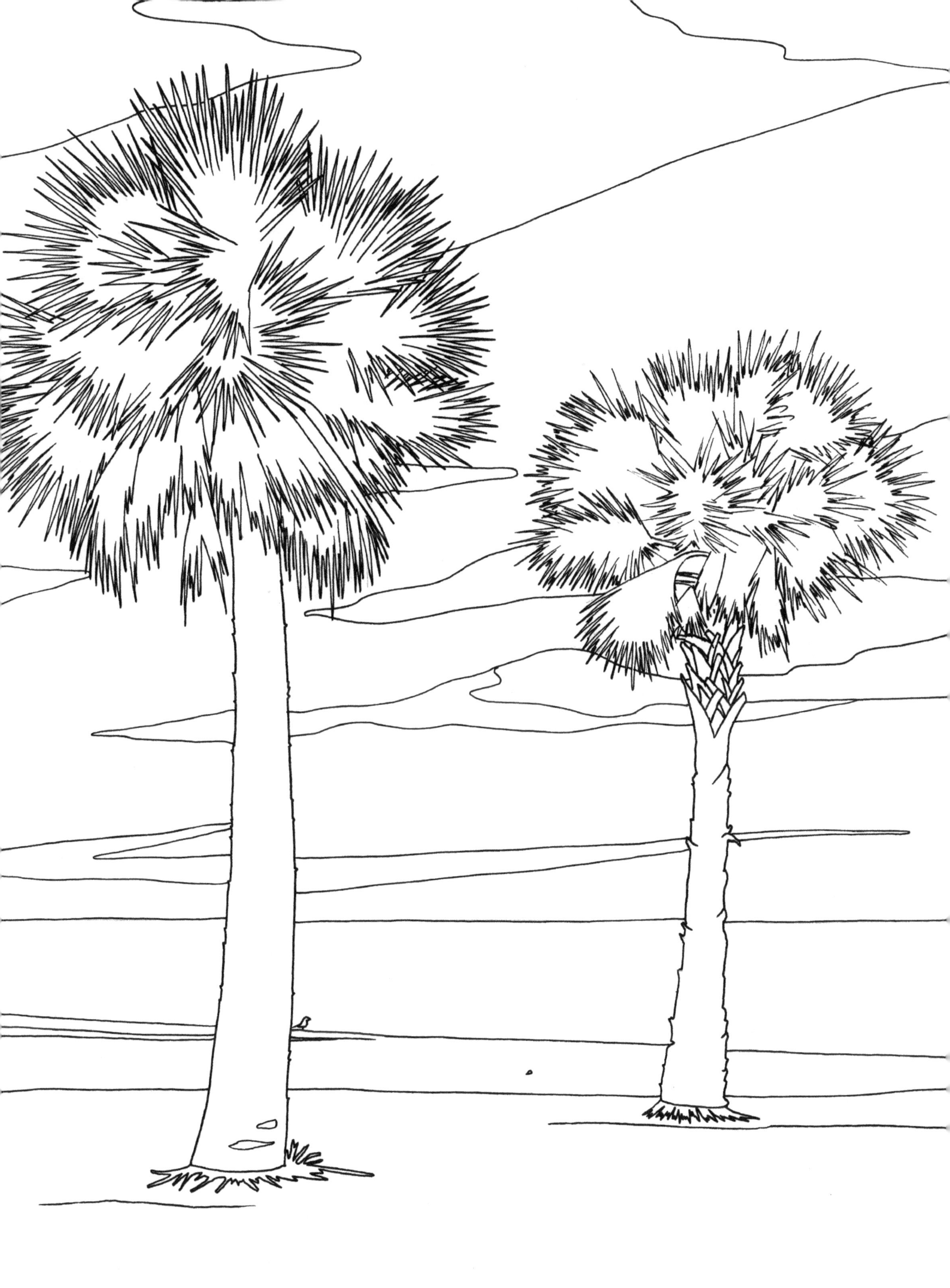

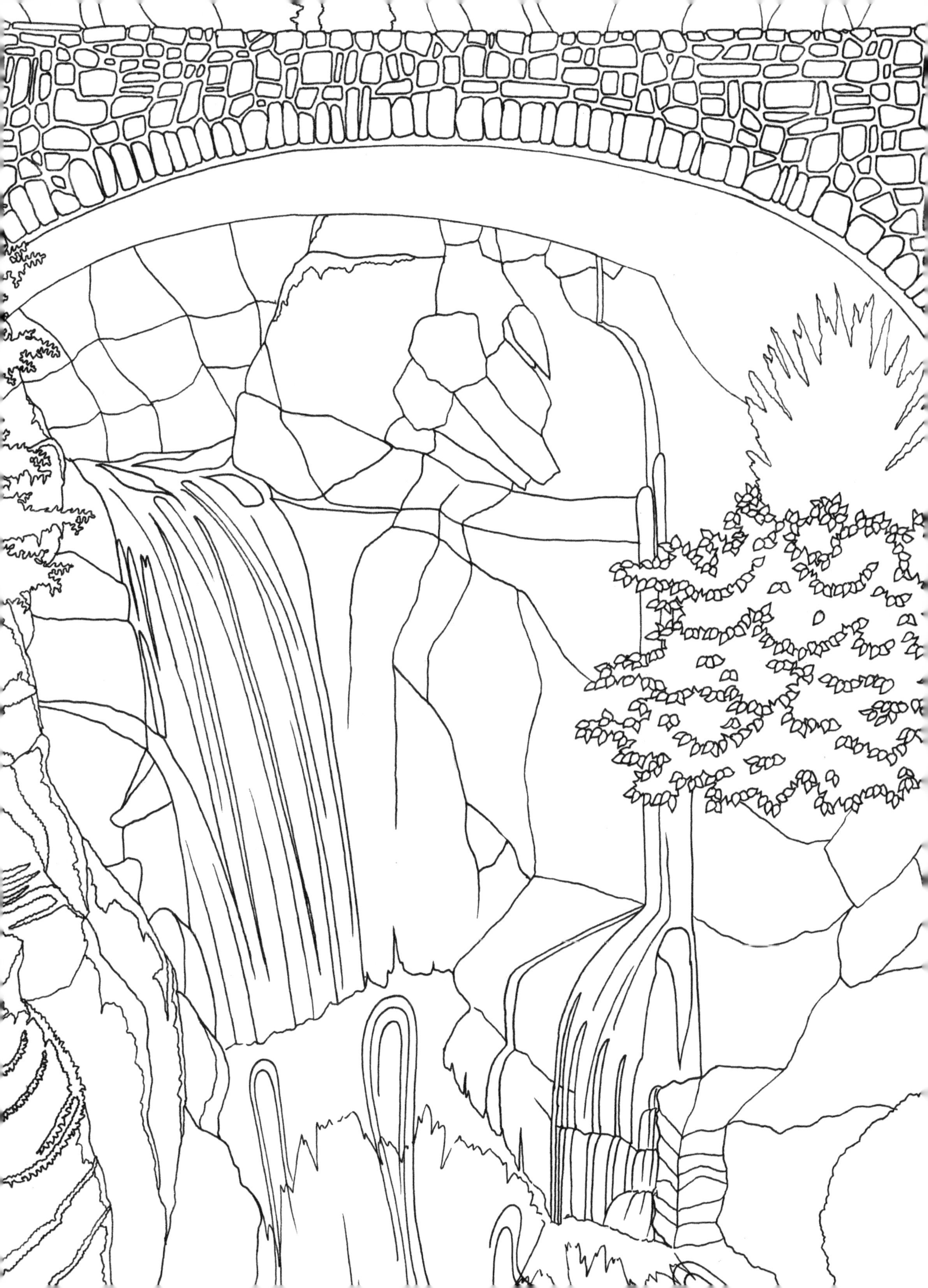

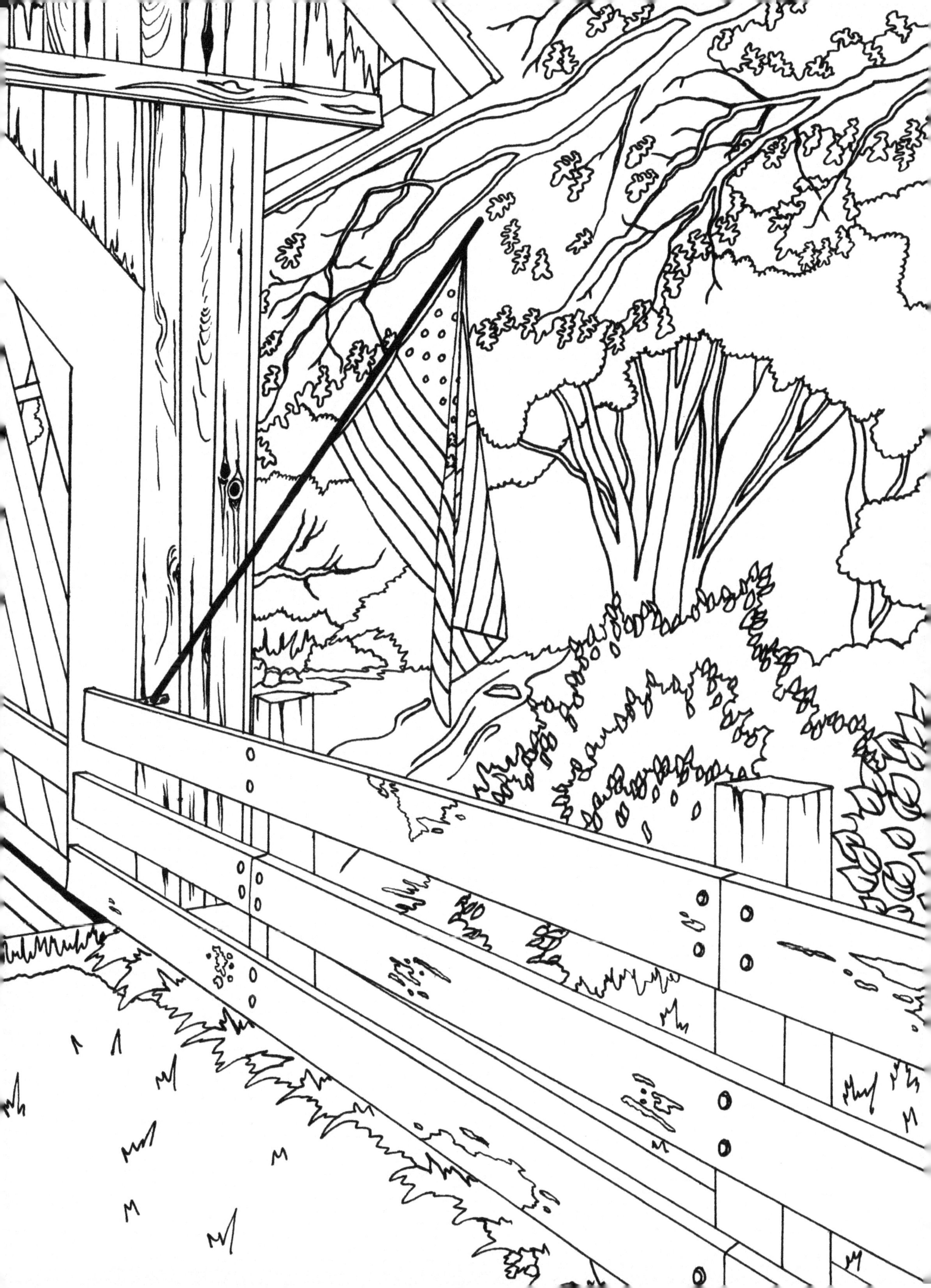

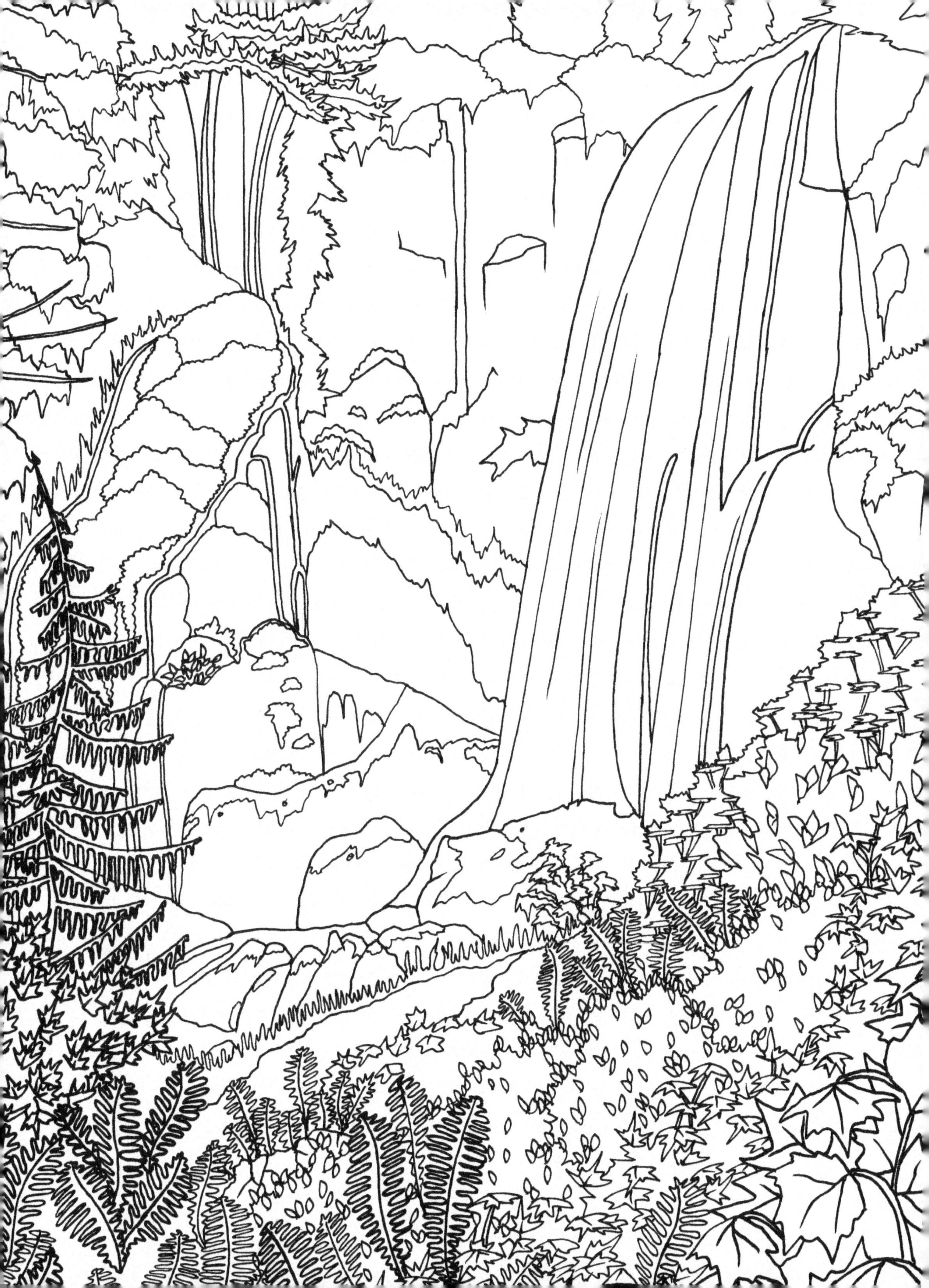

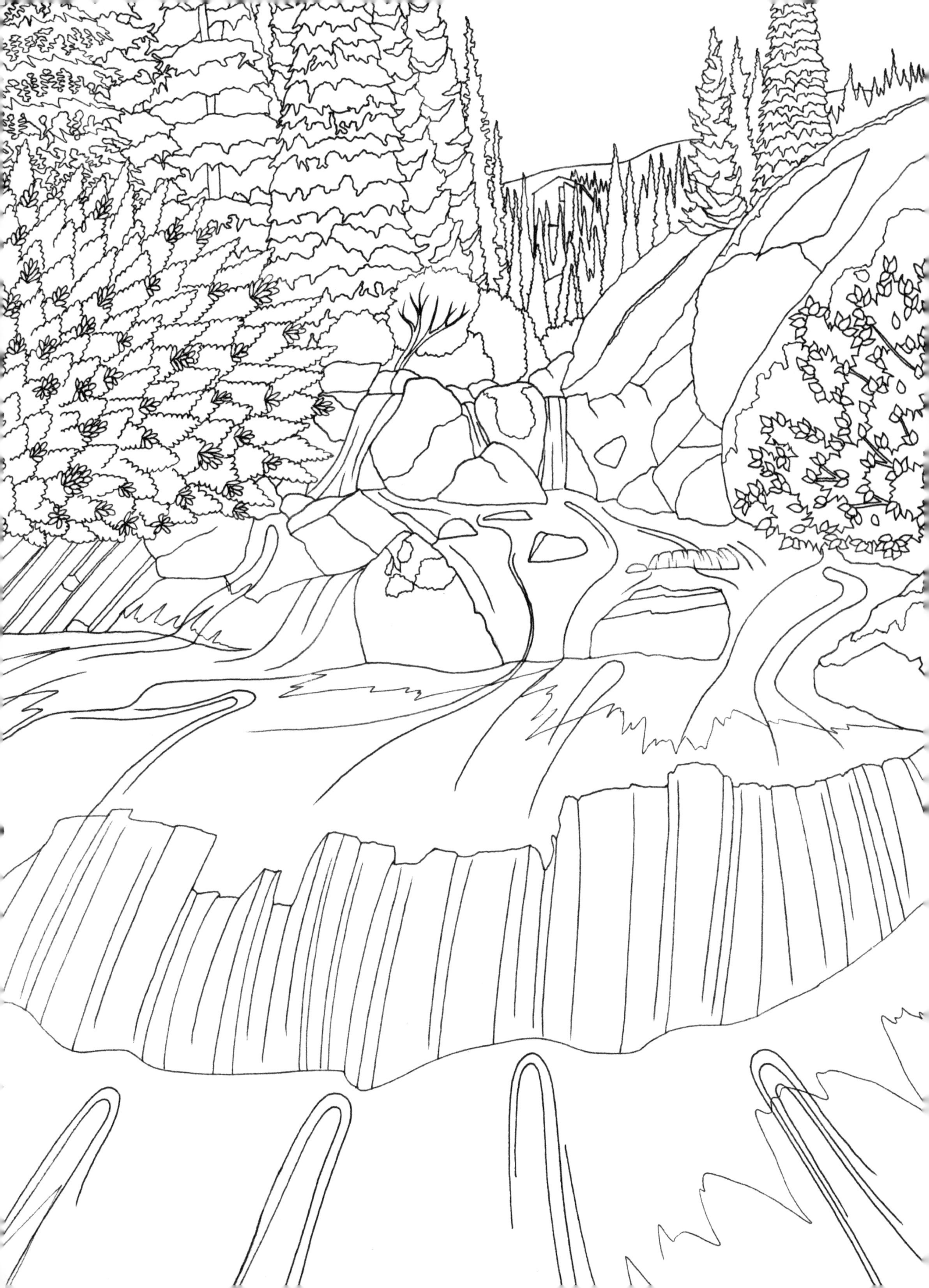

www.ingramcontent.com/pod-product-compliance
Lightning Source LLC
Chambersburg PA
CBHW040219110726
48005CB00019B/3086